1995

Merry Christmas
to
The Williams

With love's prayers!
Mary Johnston

Christmas Poems and Stories

Christmas Poems and Stories

GRAMERCY BOOKS
New York • Avenel, New Jersey

Copyright © 1992 by Outlet Book Company, Inc.,
All rights reserved

First published in 1992 by Gramercy Books,
distributed by Outlet Book Company, Inc.,
a Random House Company,
40 Engelhard Avenue
Avenel, New Jersey 07001

Manufactured in the United States

Designed by Melissa Ring

Library of Congress Cataloging-in-Publication Data
Christmas poems and stories.
p.   cm.
ISBN 0-517-08138-5
1. Christmas—Literary collections.   2. American literature.
3. English literature.   I. Gramercy Books (Firm)
PS509.C56C53.   1992   92-505
810.8′033—dc20   CIP

8   7   6   5   4   3   2   1

Contents

Introduction

Although the birthday of Jesus has been celebrated throughout the world on December 25 for more than fifteen centuries, the origins of this winter holiday extend much further back in time. Long before the birth of Christ, the Romans had a festival of tribute to Saturna, the god of plenty, from December 17 to 23 and celebrated the Birthday of the Unconquered Sun on the 25th, the day of the winter solstice. The Festival of Yule was celebrated during the same period by the Teutons in northern Europe. In the 4th century, Pope Julius I, in an attempt to absorb these and other pagan festivals into the Christian faith, decreed December 25th to be Christ's birthday, although no one knew exactly the day on which he was born.

Decorating the house with evergreens can be traced back to the Druids who used this greenery to adorn their dwellings and sacred places. Holly and ivy were long considered magical plants because they keep their leaves and bear fruit in winter, but by the Middle Ages, according to Christian teaching, holly berries came to symbolize the blood of Christ, the prickly leaves the crown of thorns and the clinging ivy immortality.

Carols originated in France. The word is from the French *carole*, meaning ring, because early carollers would dance as they sang. Although some of these early holiday songs had religious significance, most were ballads.

The tradition of Santa Claus, the jolly bringer of presents, was brought to America by Dutch settlers, who had their St. Nicholas or *Sinterklass*, for several centuries.

Today, Christmas is a wonderful amalgam of customs and traditions. It is a special, joyous time of the year when friends and families gather. It is a time of reflection and renewal, a time to sing carols, to exchange gifts, to read aloud, to share warm and generous feelings. It is hoped that this collection of Christmas poems and stories will add to your holiday pleasure this year and in many years to come.

The Angel's Story

Through the blue and frosty heavens
   Christmas stars were shining bright;
Glistening lamps throughout the city
   Almost matched their gleaming light;
While the winter snow was lying,
And the winter winds were sighing,
   Long ago, one Christmas night.

While from every tower and steeple
   Pealing bells were sounding clear,
(Never were such tones of gladness
   Save when Christmas time is near),
Many a one that night was merry
   Who had toiled through all the year.

That night saw old wrongs forgiven,
   Friends, long parted, reconciled;
Voices all unused to laughter,
   Mournful eyes that rarely smiled,
Trembling hearts that feared the morrow,
   From their anxious thoughts beguiled.

Rich and poor felt love and blessing
   From the gracious season fall;
Joy and plenty in the cottage,
   Peace and feasting in the hall;
And the voices of the children
   Ringing clear above it all!

ADELAIDE ANNE PROCTER

9

Behold, a virgin shall conceive, and bear a son, and shall call his name Immanuel. . . .

And the spirit of the Lord shall rest upon him, the spirit of wisdom and understanding, the spirit of counsel and might, the spirit of knowledge and of the fear of the Lord;

And shall make him of quick understanding in the fear of the Lord: and he shall not judge after the sight of his eyes, neither reprove after the hearing of his ears:

But with righteousness shall he judge the poor, and reprove with equity for the meek of the earth: and he shall smite the earth with the rod of his mouth, and with the breath of his lips shall he slay the wicked.

And righteousness shall be the girdle of his loins, and faithfulness the girdle of his reins.

The wolf also shall dwell with the lamb, and the leopard shall lie down with the kid; and the calf and the young lion and the fatling together; and a little child shall lead them.

Isaiah 7:14; 11:2–16

nd it came to pass in those days, that there went out a decree from Caesar Augustus, that all the world should be taxed.

(And this taxing was first made when Cyrenius was governor of Syria.)

And all went to be taxed, every one into his own city.

And Joseph also went up from Galilee, out of the city of Nazareth, into Judaea, unto the city of David, which is called Bethlehem (because he was of the house and lineage of David)

To be taxed with Mary his espoused wife, being great with child.

And so it was, that, while they were there, the days were accomplished that she should be delivered.

And she brought forth her firstborn son, and wrapped him in swaddling clothes, and laid him in a manger; because there was no room for them in the inn.

And there were in the same country shepherds abiding in the field, keeping watch over their flock by night.

And, lo, the angel of the Lord came upon them, and the glory of the Lord shone round about them: and they were sore afraid.

And the angel said unto them, Fear not: for, behold, I bring you good tidings of great joy, which shall be to all people.

For unto you is born this day in the city of David a Savior, which is Christ the Lord.

And this shall be a sign unto you; Ye shall find the babe wrapped in swaddling clothes, lying in a manger.

And suddenly there was with the angel a multitude of the heavenly host praising God, and saying,

Glory to God in the highest, and on earth peace, good will toward men.

LUKE 2:1–14

A Visit from St. Nicholas

'Twas the night before Christmas, when all through the house
Not a creature was stirring, not even a mouse.
The stockings were hung by the chimney with care,
In hopes that St. Nicholas soon would be there.
The children were nestled all snug in their beds,
While visions of sugar plums danced in their heads;
And mamma in her kerchief, and I in my cap,
Had just settled our brains for a long winter's nap—
When out on the lawn there arose such a clatter,
I sprang from my bed to see what was the matter.
Away to the window I flew like a flash,
Tore open the shutters and threw up the sash.
The moon, on the breast of the new-fallen snow,
Gave a luster of midday to objects below;
When what to my wondering eyes should appèar,

But a miniature sleigh and eight tiny reindeer,
With a little old driver, so lively and quick
I knew in a moment it must be St. Nick.
More rapid than eagles his coursers they came,
And he whistled and shouted and called them by name:
"Now, Dasher! now, Dancer! now, Prancer and Vixen!
On, Comet! on, Cupid! on, Donder and Blitzen!
To the top of the porch, to the top of the wall!
Now dash away, dash away, dash away all!"
As dry leaves that before the wild hurricane fly,
When they meet with an obstacle, mount to the sky,
So, up to the housetop the coursers they flew,
With a sleigh full of toys—and St. Nicholas too.
And then in a twinkling I heard on the roof
The prancing and pawing of each little hoof.
As I drew in my head and was turning around,
Down the chimney St. Nicholas came with a bound.

He was dressed all in fur from his head to his foot,
And his clothes were all tarnished with ashes and soot;
A bundle of toys he had flung on his back,

And he looked like a peddler just opening his pack.
His eyes, how they twinkled! his dimples, how merry!
His cheeks were like roses, his nose like a cherry;
His droll little mouth was drawn up like a bow,
And the beard on his chin was as white as the snow.
The stump of a pipe he held tight in his teeth,
And the smoke, it encircled his head like a wreath.
He had a broad face, and a little round belly
That shook, when he laughed, like a bowl full of jelly.
He was chubby and plump—a right jolly old elf—
And I laughed when I saw him, in spite of myself.
A wink of his eye and a twist of his head
Soon gave me to know I had nothing to dread.
He spoke not a word, but went straight to his work,
And filled all the stockings; then turned with a jerk,
And laying his finger aside of his nose,
And giving a nod, up the chimney he rose.
He sprang to his sleigh, to his team gave a whistle,
And away they all flew like the down of a thistle;
But I heard him exclaim, ere he drove out of sight:
"Happy Christmas to all, and to all a good night!"

CLEMENT C. MOORE

Christmas Day

A baby is a harmless thing,
   And wins our heart with one accord,
And Flower of Babies was their King,
   Jesus Christ our Lord:
Lily of lilies He
   Upon His Mother's knee;
Rose of roses, soon to be
   Crowned with thorns on leafless tree.

A lamb is innocent and mild,
   And merry on the soft green sod;
And Jesus Christ, the Undefiled,
   Is the Lamb of God:
Only spotless He
   Upon His Mother's knee;
White and ruddy, soon to be
   Sacrificed for you and me.

Nay, lamb is not so sweet a word,
   Nor lily half so pure a name;
Another name our hearts hath stirred,
   Kindling them to flame:
"Jesus" certainly
   Is music and melody:
Heart with heart in harmony
   Carol we and worship we.

CHRISTINA ROSSETTI

18

In September 1871, eight-year-old Virginia Hanlon of West 95th Street in New York City wrote the following letter to The New York *Sun*:

> Dear Editor,
>   I am eight years old. Some of my friends say there is no Santa Claus. Papa says, "If you see it in the *Sun*, it's so." Please tell me the truth, Is there a Santa Claus?

In one of the most famous editorials ever written, the editors replied:

Virginia, your little friends are wrong. They have been affected by the skepticism of a skeptical age. They do not believe except what they see. They think that nothing can be which is not comprehensible by their little minds. All minds, Virginia, whether they be men's or children's, are little. In this great universe of ours man is a mere insect, an ant, in his intellect, as compared with the boundless world about him, as measured by the intelligence capable of grasping the whole of truth and knowledge.

Yes, Virginia, there is a Santa Claus. He exists as certainly as love and generosity and devotion exist, and you know that they abound and give to your life its highest beauty and joy. Alas! how dreary would be the world if there were no Santa Claus! It would be as dreary as if there were no Virginias. There would be no childlike faith, no poetry, no romance to make tolerable this existence. We should have no enjoyment, except in sense and sight. The eternal light with which childhood fills the world would be extinguished.

Not believe in Santa Claus! You might as well not believe in fairies! You might get your papa to hire men to watch in all the chimneys on Christmas eve to catch Santa Claus, but even if they did not see Santa Claus come down, what would that prove? Nobody sees Santa Claus, but that is no sign that there is no Santa Claus. The most real things in the world are those that neither children nor men can see. Did you ever see fairies dancing on the lawn? Of course not, but that's no proof that they are not there. Nobody can conceive or imagine all the wonders there are unseen and unseeable in the world.

You tear apart the baby's rattle and see what makes the noise inside, but there is a veil covering the unseen world which not the strongest man, nor even the united strength of all the strongest men that ever lived, could tear apart. Only faith, fancy, poetry, love, romance, can push aside that curtain and view and picture the supernal beauty and glory beyond. Is it all real? Ah, Virginia, in all this world there is nothing else real and abiding.

No Santa Claus! Thank God he lives, and he lives forever. A thousand years from now, Virginia, nay, ten times ten thousand years from now, he will continue to make glad the heart of childhood.

A Christmas Eve Thought

If Santa Claus should stumble,
　　As he climbs the chimney tall
With all this ice upon it,
　　I'm afraid he'd get a fall
And smash himself to pieces—
　　To say nothing of the toys!
Dear me, what sorrow that would bring
　　To all the girls and boys!
So I am going to write a note
　　And pin it to the gate—
I'll write it large, so he can see,
　　No matter if it's late—
And say, "Dear Santa Claus, don't try
　　To climb the roof tonight,
But walk right in, the door's unlocked,
　　The nursery's on the right!"

HARRIET BREWER STERLING

CHRISTMAS GREETINGS

SHOULD YOU FIND A
    BEARDED PERSON
WITH YOUR STOCKING
    MAKING FREE,
'TWILL BE SANTA
    LEAVING WISHES
THAT ARE SIGNED AND
    SEALED BY ME.

Santa Claus lives somewhere near the North Pole, so he can't be interfered with. It is the only place where he can be sure of not being overrun with callers, who would take up all his time, and prevent him from getting his Christmas budget ready—by no means a light piece of work. As to how he makes up his load of toys, it is certainly curious; but it is his business not ours. He uses reindeer to draw his sleigh because no other animals can endure the climate in which their master must live. Just what Santa looks like is not altogether certain, but there is a belief among the children who have sat up to receive his visits that he is not so big but that he can get through an ordinary chimney; that he is compelled to dress in furs because of the cold ride through the long winter night; that he looks good-natured because no one that loves young folk can help looking so; and that his beard and his hair are white because he is older by some years than he was in his younger days. He must be a jolly and kindly old gentleman, for otherwise he wouldn't be giving out his toys in that sly, queer way of his—after the little ones are fast asleep and snug in their beds. Oh, we can tell quite a number of things about his tricks and his manners! But don't sit up for him; he doesn't like it. He loses valuable time when he is compelled to dodge the prying eyes of little Susan Sly and Master Paul Pry, and so kindly an old fellow should not be bothered. Just go to bed, close your eyes up good and tight, and—see what you will find in the morning!

From *St. Nicholas* Magazine

The Holly and the Ivy

The holly and the ivy,
When they are both full grown,
Of all the trees that are in the wood,
The holly bears the crown.

The rising of the sun
And the running of the deer,
The playing of the merry organ,
Sweet singing in the choir.

The holly bears a blossom
As white as the lily flower,
And Mary bore sweet Jesus Christ
To be our sweet savior.

The holly bears a berry
As red as any blood,
And Mary bore sweet Jesus Christ
To do poor sinners good.

The holly bears a prickle
As sharp as any thorn,
And Mary bore sweet Jesus Christ
On Christmas day in the morn.

The holly bears a bark
As bitter as any gall,
And Mary bore sweet Jesus Christ
For to redeem us all.

The holly and the ivy,
When they are both full grown,
Of all the trees that are in the wood
The holly bears the crown.

OLD ENGLISH CAROL

Where Is This Stupendous Stranger?

Where is this stupendous stranger?
Swains of Solyma, advise,
Lead me to my Master's manger,
Show me where my Savior lies.

Nature's decorations glisten
Far above their usual trim;
Birds on box and laurel listen,
As so near the cherubs hymn.

God all-bounteous, all-creative,
Whom no ills from good dissuade,
Is incarnate, and a native
Of the very world He made.

CHRISTOPHER SMART

On Christmas Day

On Christmas Day, when fires were lit,
 And all our breakfasts done,
We spread our toys out on the floor
 And played there in the sun.

The nursery smelled of Christmas tree,
 And under where it stood
The shepherds watched their flocks of sheep,
 —All made of painted wood.

Outside the house the air was cold
 And quiet all about,
Till far across the snowy roofs
 The Christmas bells rang out.

But soon the sleigh bells jingled by
 Upon the street below,
And people on the way to church,
 Went crunching through the snow.

We did not quarrel once all day;
 Mama and Grandma said
They liked to be in where we were,
 So pleasantly we played.

I do not see how any child
 Is cross on Christmas day,
When all the lovely toys are new,
 And everyone can play.

KATHARINE PYLE

I have been looking at a merry company of children assembled round that pretty German toy, a Christmas tree. The tree was planted in the middle of a great round table and towered high above their heads. It was brilliantly lighted by a multitude of little tapers; and everywhere sparkled and glittered with bright objects. There were rosy-cheeked dolls, hiding behind the green leaves; and there were real watches (with movable hands, at least, and an endless capacity of being wound up) dangling from innumerable twigs; there were French-polished tables, chairs, bedsteads, wardrobes, eight-day clocks, and various other articles of domestic furniture (wonderfully made in tin), perched among the boughs, as if in preparation for some fairy housekeeping; there were jolly, broad-faced little men, much more agreeable in appearance than many real men—and no wonder, for their heads took off, and showed them to be full of sugarplums; there were trinkets for the elder girls, far brighter than any grown-up gold and jewels; there were baskets and pincushions in all devices; there were guns, swords, and banners; there were witches standing in enchanted rings of pasteboard, to tell fortunes; there were teetotums, humming tops, needle cases, pen wipers, smelling bottles, conversation cards, bouquet holders; real fruit, made artificially dazzling with gold leaf; imitation apples, pears, and walnuts crammed with surprises; in short, as a pretty child, before me, delightedly whispered to another pretty child, her bosom friend, "There was everything, and more."

From A *Christmas Tree* by CHARLES DICKENS

A Merry Christmas

She had a splendid Christmas. She went to bed early, so as to let Santa Claus have a chance at the stockings, and in the morning she was up the first of anybody and went and felt them, and found hers all lumpy with packages of candy, and oranges and grapes, and pocketbooks and rubber balls and all kinds of small presents, and her big brother's with nothing but the tongs in them, and her young lady sister's with a new silk umbrella, and her papa's and mama's with potatoes and pieces of coal wrapped up in tissue paper, just as they always had every Christmas. Then she waited around till the rest of the family were up, and she was the first to burst into the library, when the doors were opened, and look at the large presents laid out on the library table—books, and portfolios, and boxes of stationery, and breast pins, and dolls, and little stoves, and dozens of handkerchiefs, and inkstands, and skates, and snow shovels, and photograph frames, and little easels, and boxes of watercolors, and Turkish paste, and nougat, and candied cherries, and dolls' houses, and waterproofs—and the big Christmas tree lighted and standing in a wastebasket in the middle.

She had a splendid Christmas all day. She ate so much candy that she did not want any breakfast; and the whole forenoon the presents kept pouring in that the expressman had not had time to deliver the night before; and she went 'round giving the presents she had got for other people, and came home and ate turkey and cranberry for dinner, and plum pudding and nuts and raisins and oranges and more candy, and then went out and coasted and came in with a stomachache.

From *Christmas Every Day* by WILLIAM DEAN HOWELLS

The Gift of the Magi

One dollar and eighty-seven cents. That was all. And sixty cents of it was in pennies. Pennies saved one and two at a time by bulldozing the grocer and the vegetable man and the butcher until one's cheeks burned with the silent imputation of parsimony that such close dealing implied. Three times Della counted it. One dollar and eighty-seven cents. And the next day would be Christmas.

There was clearly nothing to do but flop down on the shabby little couch and howl. So Della did it. Which instigates the moral reflection that life is made up of sobs, sniffles, and smiles, with sniffles predominating.

While the mistress of the home is gradually subsiding from the first stage to the second, take a look at the home. A furnished flat at eight dollars per week. It did not exactly beggar description, but it certainly had that word on the lookout for the mendicancy squad.

In the vestibule below was a letter box into which no letter would go, and an electric button from which no mortal finger could coax a ring. Also appertaining thereunto was a card bearing the name "Mr. James Dillingham Young."

The "Dillingham" had been flung to the breeze during a former period of prosperity when its possessor was being paid thirty dollars per week. Now, when the income was shrunk to twenty dollars, the letters of "Dillingham" looked blurred, as though they were thinking seriously of contracting to a modest and unassuming D. But whenever Mr. James Dillingham Young came home and reached his flat above he was called "Jim" and greatly hugged by Mrs. James Dillingham Young, already introduced to you as Della. Which is all very good.

Della finished her cry and attended to her cheeks with the powder rag. She stood by the window and looked out dully at a gray cat walking a gray fence in a gray backyard. Tomorrow would be Christmas Day, and she had only one dollar and eighty-seven cents with which to buy Jim a present. She had been saving every penny she could for months, with this result. Twenty dollars a week doesn't go far. Expenses had been greater than she had calculated. They always are. Only one dollar and eighty-seven cents to buy a present for Jim. Her Jim. Many a happy hour she had spent planning for something nice for him. Something fine and rare and sterling—something just a little bit near to being worthy of the honor of being owned by Jim.

There was a pier glass between the windows of the room. Perhaps you have seen a pier glass in an eight-dollar flat. A very thin and very agile person may, by observing his reflection in a rapid sequence of longitudinal strips, obtain a fairly accurate conception of his looks. Della, being slender, had mastered the art.

Suddenly she whirled from the window and stood before the glass. Her eyes were shining brilliantly, but her face had lost its color within twenty seconds. Rapidly she pulled down her hair and let it fall to its full length.

Now, there were two possessions of the James Dillingham Youngs in which they both took a mighty pride. One was Jim's gold watch that had been his father's and grandfather's. The other was Della's hair. Had the Queen of Sheba lived in the flat across the airshaft, Della would have let her hair hang out the window some day to dry just to depreciate her majesty's jewels and gifts. Had King Solomon been the janitor, with all his treasures piled up in the basement, Jim would have pulled out his watch every time he passed, just to see him pluck at his beard from envy.

So now Della's beautiful hair fell about her, rippling and shining like a cascade of brown waters. It reached below her knee and made itself almost a garment for her. And then she did it up again nervously and quickly. Once she faltered for a minute and stood still while a tear or two splashed on the worn red carpet.

On went her old brown jacket; on went her old brown hat. With a whirl of skirts and with the brilliant sparkle still in her eyes, she fluttered out the door and down the stairs to the street.

Where she stopped the sign read: "Mme. Sofronie. Hair Goods of All Kinds." One flight up Della ran, and collected herself, panting. Madame, large, too white, chilly, hardly looked the "Sofronie."

"Will you buy my hair?" asked Della.

"I buy hair," said Madame. "Take yer hat off and let's have a sight at the looks of it."

Down rippled the brown cascade.

"Twenty dollars," said Madame, lifting the mass with a practiced hand.

"Give it to me quick," said Della.

Oh, and the next two hours tripped by on rosy wings. Forget the hashed metaphor. She was ransacking the stores for Jim's present.

She found it at last. It surely had been made for Jim and no one else. There was no other like it in any of the stores, and she had turned all of them inside out. It was a platinum fob chain simple and chaste in design, properly proclaiming its value by substance alone and not by meretricious ornamentation—as all good things should do. It was even worthy of The Watch. As soon as she saw it she knew that it must be Jim's. It was like him. Quietness and value—the description applied to both. Twenty-one dollars they took from her for it, and she hurried home with the eighty-seven cents. With that chain on his watch Jim might be properly anxious about the time in any company. Grand as the watch was, he sometimes looked at it on the sly on account of the old leather strap that he used in place of a chain.

When Della reached home her intoxication gave way a little to prudence and reason. She got out her curling irons and lighted the gas and went to work repairing the ravages made by generosity added to love. Which is always a tremendous task, dear friends—a mammoth task.

Within forty minutes her head was covered with tiny, close-lying curls that made her look wonderfully like a truant schoolboy. She looked at her reflection in the mirror long, carefully, and critically.

"If Jim doesn't kill me," she said to herself, "before he takes a second look at me, he'll say I look like a Coney Island chorus girl. But what could I do—oh! what could I do with a dollar and eighty-seven cents?"

At seven o'clock the coffee was made and the frying pan was on the back of the stove and ready to cook the chops.

Jim was never late. Della doubled the fob chain in her hand and sat on the corner of the table near the door that he always entered. Then she heard his step on the stair away down on the first flight, and she turned white for just a moment. She had a habit of saying little silent prayers about the simplest everyday things, and now she whispered: "Please God, make him think I am still pretty."

The door opened and Jim stepped in and closed it. He looked thin and very serious. Poor fellow, he was only twenty-two—and to be burdened with a family! He needed a new overcoat and he was without gloves.

Jim stopped inside the door, as immovable as a setter at the scent of quail. His eyes were fixed upon Della, and there was an expression in them that she could not read, and it terrified her. It was not anger, nor surprise, nor disapproval, nor horror, nor any of the sentiments that she had been prepared for. He simply stared at her fixedly with that peculiar expression on his face.

Della wriggled off the table and went for him.

"Jim, darling," she cried, "don't look at me that way. I had my hair cut off and sold it because I couldn't have lived through Christmas without giving you a present. It'll grow out again—

you won't mind, will you? I just had to do it. My hair grows awfully fast. Say 'Merry Christmas!' Jim, and let's be happy. You don't know what a nice—what a beautiful, nice gift I've got for you."

"You've cut off your hair?" asked Jim, laboriously, as if he had not arrived at that patent fact yet even after the hardest mental labor.

"Cut it off and sold it," said Della. "Don't you like me just as well, anyhow? I'm me without my hair, ain't I?"

Jim looked about the room curiously.

"You say your hair is gone?" he said, with an air almost of idiocy.

"You needn't look for it," said Della. "It's sold, I tell you—sold and gone, too. It's Christmas Eve, boy. Be good to me, for it went for you. Maybe the hairs of my head were numbered," she went on with a sudden serious sweetness, "but nobody could ever count my love for you. Shall I put the chops on, Jim?"

Out of his trance Jim seemed quickly to wake. He enfolded his Della. For ten seconds let us regard with discreet scrutiny some inconsequential object in the other direction. Eight dollars a week or a million a year—what is the difference? A mathematician or a wit would give you the wrong answer. The magi brought valuable gifts, but that was not among them. This dark assertion will be illuminated later on.

Jim drew a package from his overcoat pocket and threw it upon the table.

"Don't make any mistake, Dell," he said, "about me. I don't think there's anything in the way of a haircut or a shave or a shampoo that could make me like my girl any less. But if you'll unwrap that package you may see why you had me going a while at first."

White fingers and nimble tore at the string and paper. And then an ecstatic scream of joy; and then, alas! a quick feminine change to hysterical tears and wails, necessitating the immediate employment of all the comforting powers of the lord of the flat.

For there lay The Combs—the set of combs, side and back, that Della had worshiped for long in a Broadway window. Beau-

40

tiful combs, pure tortoise shell, with jeweled rims—just the shade to wear in the beautiful vanished hair. They were expensive combs, she knew, and her heart had simply craved and yearned over them without the least hope of possession. And now, they were hers, but the tresses that should have adorned the coveted adornments were gone.

But she hugged them to her bosom, and at length she was able to look up with dim eyes and a smile and say: "My hair grows so fast, Jim!"

And then Della leaped up like a little singed cat and cried, "Oh, oh!"

Jim had not yet seen his beautiful present. She held it out to him eagerly upon her open palm. The dull precious metal seemed to flash with a reflection of her bright and ardent spirit.

"Isn't it a dandy, Jim? I hunted all over town to find it. You'll have to look at the time a hundred times a day now. Give me your watch. I want to see how it looks on it."

Instead of obeying, Jim tumbled down on the couch and put his hands under the back of his head and smiled.

"Dell," said he, "let's put our Christmas presents away and keep 'em a while. They're too nice to use just at present. I sold the watch to get the money to buy your combs. And now suppose you put the chops on."

The magi, as you know, were wise men—wonderfully wise men who brought gifts to the Babe in the manger. They invented the art of giving Christmas presents. Being wise, their gifts were no doubt wise ones, possibly bearing the privilege of exchange in case of duplication. And here I have lamely related to you the uneventful chronicle of two foolish children in a flat who most unwisely sacrificed for each other the greatest treasures of their house. But in a last word to the wise of these days let it be said that of all who give gifts these two were the wisest. Of all who give and receive gifts, such as they are wisest. Everywhere they are wisest. They are the magi.

O. Henry

A Christmas Countdown

Ten Christmas presents standing in a line;

Robert took the bicycle, then there were nine.

Nine Christmas presents ranged in order straight;

Bob took the steam engine, then there were eight.

Eight Christmas presents—and one came from Devon;

Robbie took the jackknife, then there were seven.

Seven Christmas presents direct from St. Nick's;

Bobby took the candy box, then there were six.

Six Christmas presents, one of them alive;

Rob took the puppy dog, then there were five.

Five Christmas presents yet on the floor;

Bobbin took the soldier cap, then there were four.

Four Christmas presents underneath the tree;

Bobbet took the writing desk, then there were three.

Three Christmas presents still in full view;

Robin took the checker board, then there were two.

Two Christmas presents, promising fun,

Bobbles took the picture book, and there was one.

One Christmas present—and now the list is done;

Bobbinet took the sled, and then there were none.

And the same happy child received every toy,

So many nicknames had one little boy.

CAROLYN WELLS

Good King Wenceslas

Good King Wenceslas looked out
On the Feast of Stephen,
When the snow lay round about,
Deep and crisp and even:
Brightly shone the moon that night,
Though the frost was cruel,
When a poor man came in sight,
Gath'ring winter fuel.

"Hither, page, and stand by me,
If thou know'st it, telling:
Yonder peasant, who is he?
Where and what his dwelling?"
"Sire, he lives a good league hence,
Underneath the mountain;
Right against the forest fence,
By Saint Agnes' fountain."

"Bring me flesh and bring me wine,
Bring me pine logs hither;
Thou and I will see him dine,
When we bear them thither,"
Page and monarch forth they went,
Forth they went together;
Through the rude wind's wild lament,
And the bitter weather.

"Sire, the night is darker now,
And the wind blows stronger;
Fails my heart, I know not how,
I can go no longer."
"Mark my footsteps, my good page,
Tread thou in them boldly:
Thou shalt find the winter's rage,
Freeze thy blood less coldly."

In his master's steps he trod,
Where the snow lay dinted;
Heat was in the very sod
Which the saint had printed.
Therefore, Christian men, be sure,
Wealth or rank possessing,
"Ye who now will bless the poor,
Shall yourselves find blessing."

Merry Christmas, Everyone!

In the rush of the merry morning,
   When the red burns through the gray,
And the wintry world lies waiting
   For the glory of the day,
Then we hear a fitful rushing
   Just without, upon the stair,
See two white phantoms coming,
   Catch the gleam of sunny hair.

Rosy feet upon the threshold,
   Eager faces peeping through,
With the first red ray of sunshine
   Chanting cherubs come in view;
Mistletoe and gleaming holly,
   Symbols of a blessed day,
In their chubby hands they carry,
   Streaming all along the way.

Well we know them, never weary
   Of their innocent surprise;
Waiting, watching, listening always
   With full hearts and tender eyes,
While our little household angels,
   White and golden in the sun.
Greet us with the sweet old welcome—
   "Merry Christmas, everyone!"

AUTHOR UNKNOWN

M for the **M**usic, merry and clear;

E for the **E**ve, the crown of the year;

R for the **R**omping of bright girls and boys;

R for the **R**eindeer that bring them the toys;

Y for the **Y**ule-log softly aglow.

C for the **C**old of the sky and the snow;

H for the **H**earth where they hang up the hose;

R for the **R**eel which the old folk propose;

I for the **I**cicles seen through the pane;

S for the **S**leigh-bells, with tinkling refrain;

T for the **T**ree with gifts all a-bloom;

M for the **M**istletoe hung in the room;

A for the **A**nthems we all love to hear;

S for **S**t. Nicholas—joy of the year!

AUTHOR UNKNOWN

Christmas

Dark and dull night fly hence away
And give the honor to this day
That sees December turn'd to May.

Why does the chilling winter's morn
Smile like a field beset with corn?
Or smell like a mead new-shorn
Thus on the sudden?—Come and see
The cause why things thus fragrant be.

ROBERT HERRICK

Christmas Bells

I heard the bells on Christmas Day
Their old familiar carols play,
  And wild and sweet
  The word repeat
Of peace on earth, good will to men!

And thought how, as the day had come,
The belfries of all Christendom
  Had rolled along
  The unbroken song
Of peace on earth, good will to men!

Till, ringing, swinging on its way,
The world revolved from night to day
  A voice, a chime,
  A chant sublime
Of peace on earth, good will to men!

Then from each black, accursed mouth
The cannon thundered in the South
  And with the sound
  The carols drowned
Of peace on earth, good will to men!

It was as if an earthquake rent
The hearthstones of a continent,
And made forlorn
The households born
Of peace on earth, good will to men!

And in despair I bowed my head;
"There is no peace on earth," I said;
For hate is strong
And mocks the song
Of peace on earth, good will to men!"

Then pealed the bells more loud and deep,
"God is not dead; nor doth He sleep!
The Wrong shall fail,
The Right prevail,
With peace on earth, good will to men!"

HENRY WADSWORTH LONGFELLOW

The Christmas Dinner

Lo now is come the joyful'st feast!
Let every man be jolly.
Each room with ivy leaves is dress'd,
And every post with holly.
Now all our neighbors' chimneys smoke
And Christmas blocks are burning;
Their ovens they with bak't meats choke
And all their spits are turning.
Without the door let sorrow lie,
And if, for cold, it hap to die,
We'll bury't in a Christmas pie
And evermore be merry.

AUTHOR UNKNOWN

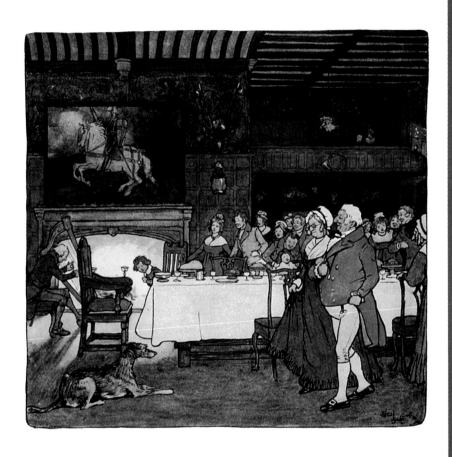

The Worcestershire Carol

How grand and how bright
That wonderful night
When angels to Bethlehem came.
They burst forth like fires
They struck their gold lyres
And mingled their sound with the flame.

The shepherds were amazed
The pretty lambs gazed
At darkness thus turned into light.
No voice was there heard
From man, beast or bird
So sudden and solemn the sight.

And then when the sound
Re-echoed around
The hills and the dales all awoke.
The moon and the stars
Stopt their fiery ears
And listened while Gabriel spoke.

"I bring you," said he,
"From the glorious tree,
A message both gladsome and good.
The Savior is come
To the world as His home
But He lies in a manger of wood."

At the mention of this
The source of all bliss
The angels sang loudly and long.
They soared to the sky
Beyond mortal eye
But left us the words of their song:

"All glory to God
Who laid by His rod
To smile on the world through His Son.
And peace be on earth
For this holy birth
Most wonderful conquests has won."

ENGLISH CAROL

 55

"Merry Christmas" Around the World

Boas Festas y Feliz Ano Novo
PORTUGESE

God Jul
SWEDISH

Boze Narodzenie
POLISH

S Rozhdestvom Kristovym
RUSSIAN

Nodlaig Mhaith Chugnat IRISH

Sarbatori Vesele
RUMANIAN

Chrystos Rozdzajetsia Slawyte Jeho
UKRAINIAN

Nadolig Llawen
WELSH

Kellemes Karacsonyi Unnepeket
HUNGARIAN

Vesele Vianoce
SLOVAKIAN

Glaedelig Jul
DANISH

Sretan Bozic
CROATIAN

Noeliniz Ve Yeni Yiliniz Kutlu Olsun
TURKISH

Buon Natale
ITALIAN

 56

Schernorhavor Dzenount
ARMENIAN

Linksmu Kaledu
LITHUANIAN

Cestitamo Bozic
YUGOSLAVIAN

Vesele Vanoce
BOHEMIAN

Joyeux Noël
FRENCH

Houska Joulua
FINNISH

Chestita Koleda
BULGARIAN

Kala Christougena
GREEK

Vrolyk Kerfeest en Gelukkig Nieuw Jaar
DUTCH

Hristos Se Rodi
SERBIAN

God Jul og Godt Nytt Aar
NORWEGIAN

Feliz Navidad
SPANISH

Vrolike Kerstmis
FLEMISH

Een Plesierige Kerfees
AFRIKANER

Froehliche Weihnachten
GERMAN

 57

A Christmas Alphabet

A   is for Animals who shared the stable.

B   is for the Babe with their manger for cradle.

C   is for the Carols so blithe and so gay.

D   for December, the twenty-fifth day.

E   for the Eve when we're all so excited.

F   for the Fun when the tree's at last lighted.

G   is the Goose which you all know is fat.

H   for the Holly you stick in your hat.

I   for the Ivy that clings to the wall.

J   is for Jesus, the cause of it all.

K   for the Kindness begot by this feast.

L   is the Light shining way in the east.

M   for the Mistletoe, all green and white.

N   for the Noëls we sing Christmas night.

O for the Oxen, the first to adore Him.

P for the Presents Wise Men laid before Him.

Q for the Queerness that this should have been
Near two thousand years before you were seen.

R for the Reindeer leaping the roofs.

S for the Stockings that Santa Claus stuffs.

T for the Toys, the Tinsel, the Tree.

U is for Us—the whole family.

V is for Visitors bringing us cheer.

W is Welcome to the happy New Year.

X Y Z bother me! All I can say,
Is this is the end of my Christmas lay.
So now to you all, wherever you be,
A merry, merry Christmas, and many may you see!

AUTHOR UNKNOWN

Nearer and closer to our hearts be the Christmas spirit, which is the spirit of active usefulness, perseverance, cheerful discharge of duty, kindness, and forbearance.

CHARLES DICKENS

May each Christmas, as it comes, find us more and more like Him who at this time became a little child, for our sake; more simple-minded, more humble, more affectionate, more resigned, more happy, more full of God.

JOHN HENRY, CARDINAL NEWMAN

crooge was early at the office next morning. Oh, he was early there! If he could only be there first, and catch Bob Cratchit coming late! That was the thing he had set his heart upon.

And he did it; yes, he did! The clock struck nine. No Bob. A quarter past. No Bob. He was a full eighteen minutes and a half behind his time. Scrooge sat with his door wide open, that he might see him come into the tank.

His hat was off before he opened the door; his comforter too. He was on his stool in a jiffy, driving away with his pen, as if he were trying to overtake nine o'clock.

"Hallo!" growled Scrooge in his accustomed voice as near as he could feign it. "What do you mean by coming here at this time of day?"

"I am very sorry, sir," said Bob. "I *am* behind my time."

"You are!" repeated Scrooge. "Yes, I think you are. Step this way, sir, if you please."

"It's only once a year, sir," pleaded Bob, appearing from the tank. "It shall not be repeated. I was making rather merry yesterday, sir."

"Now, I'll tell you what, my friend," said Scrooge. "I am not going to stand this sort of thing any longer. And therefore," he continued, leaping from his stool, and giving Bob such a dig in the waistcoat that he staggered back into the tank again—"and therefore I am about to . . . raise your salary!"

Bob trembled, and got a little nearer to the ruler. He had a momentary idea of knocking Scrooge down with it, holding him, and calling to the people in the court for help and a strait-waistcoat.

"A merry Christmas, Bob!" said Scrooge, with an earnestness that could not be mistaken, as he clapped him on the back. "A merrier Christmas, Bob, my good fellow, than I have given you for many a year! I'll raise your salary, and endeavor to assist your struggling family, and we will discuss your affairs this very afternoon, over a Christmas bowl of smoking bishop, Bob! Make up the fires and buy another coal-scuttle before you dot another *i*, Bob Cratchit!"

Scrooge was better than his word; he did it all, and infinitely more. And to Tiny Tim, who did *not* die, he was a second father. He became as good a friend, as good a master, and as good a man as the good old City knew, or any other good old city, town, or borough in the good old world. . . . And it was always said of him that he knew how to keep Christmas well, if any man alive possessed the knowledge. May that be truly said of us, and all of us!

And so, as Tiny Tim observed, God Bless Us, Every One!

From *A Christmas Carol* by CHARLES DICKENS

A bright and happy Christmas.